PIANO SOLOS
THE BEST OF

JELLY ROLL
MORTON

Cover photo courtesy of:
Photographs and Prints Division
Schomburg Center for Research in Black Culture
The New York Public Library
Astor, Lenox and Tilden Foundations

ISBN 978-0-7935-2063-3

HAL•LEONARD®
CORPORATION
7777 W. BLUEMOUND RD. P.O. BOX 13819 MILWAUKEE, WI 53213

"THE INVENTOR OF JAZZ"

Born Ferdinand Joseph La Menthe on September 20, 1885, Jelly Roll Morton was a New Orleans Creole – of mixed African-American and European heritage. The surname Morton came from the man his mother married when he was three.

As music was an intrinsic part of New Orleans life, it became an intrinsic part of Morton's childhood. Influences came from the music of the street parades and funerals, the opera, his father Ferdinand P. La Menthe's trombone playing, and later on, the places in which he performed, such as Storyville's sporting houses (brothels), nightclubs and eventually vaudeville, not only as a pianist but on guitar, trombone, drums and also as a singer. Inspiration came from one of Morton's mentors, singer/pianist Tony Jackson, who had extraordinarily wide musical tastes and put an emphasis on writing down his music, clearly outlining his plans for recording dates, and publishing his arrangements – lessons Morton learned well.

Many of Morton's best-known pieces – "New Orleans Blues," "King Porter Stomp," "Jelly Roll Blues" and "The Wolverines (Wolverine Blues)" – he composed in New Orleans while still in his teens. During this period, Morton began using the word *jazz*, more as a verb as *to jazz up* and change music, and he made the distinction very clear between jazz, blues and ragtime. He saw the latter two as very structured – in rhythm, form and chord progressions – whereas jazz had an improvisational nature.

It was Morton's job as a sporting house pianist, at the age of 17, that caused his eviction from his home and started him traveling, leaving New Orleans forever. Like a gypsy, he would set up "camp" in a city (Chicago, Memphis, Mobile, St. Louis, New York, Tulsa) for a short while, and then travel on. Morton's musical impact was immediate and memorable: the first wide-ranging reports of hearing "Jelly Roll Blues" were made by pianist George W. Smith in Texas and the legendary composer/pianist James P. Johnson in New York.* Critics noted the difference in Morton's (jazz) sound and the prevailing popular sound of ragtime. Accounts from this period raved about Morton's pianistic prowess, but also took note of his ability to transform the idiom of blues solos into the wider format of instrumental ensemble blues.

Morton lived in Los Angeles from 1917 to 1923, where he became involved romantically with Anita Johnson Gonzales, whose writing credit appears on "Dead Man Blues." But no matter where he was, each composition added an innovation, such as the "break," which was heard early in "Jelly Roll Blues" and "New Orleans Blues," and evidence of Morton's skill at instrumental composition, which showed in such keyboard compositions as "Chicago Breakdown," "Wild Man Blues (Ted Lewis Blues)" and "Grandpa's Spells," with breaks phrased as if they were written for wind instruments.

Morton's work was popular among his peers. King Oliver and his Creole Jazz Band (with Louis Armstrong on the early recordings) played or recorded "Mister Joe," "Frog-I-More" and "London Café Blues (London Blues)," as well as a duo of "King Porter Stomp" with Morton on piano and Oliver on cornet in 1924.

While Morton was in Chicago in 1923, he hooked up with Melrose Brothers Music, which assisted him in getting recording deals. Notable in 1923 were the Gennett Records' solo sessions where Morton put down six high-quality sides, including "King Porter Stomp," "New Orleans Blues," "Grandpa's Spells," "The Wolverines (Wolverine Blues)" and "The Pearls," one of his most challenging pieces. In later solo sessions in 1924, he recorded "Shreveport Stomp," "Stratford Hunch" and "Jelly Roll Blues." Also on Gennett, with the New Orleans Rhythm Kings, he recorded "Mr. Jelly-Lord," the soon-to-be-famous "Milenberg Joys," and "London Blues," a tune he recorded four times (the last in 1928 with the Red Hot Peppers as "Shoe Shiner's Drag").

Morton's biggest recording deal was with Victor, which had its first major hits in 1926 and 1927 with Morton's Red Hot Peppers band. (The word "hot" was often the record company's adjective for jazz.) Alan Lomax called these "the finest recordings of New Orleans music ever made."* Many of the pieces heard on these recordings were arrangements of piano compositions – arrangements that often turned corners on their original structure, sometimes resulting in alternate titles. The success of these recordings was due to Morton's meticulous planning – most of the arrangements were written out, the band was rehearsed and Morton conferred with the musicians on their solos.

"Black Bottom Stomp (Queen Of Spades)," from the first of these sessions, incorporated all of the Morton specialties in rhythmic, improvisational and thematic forms, textural contrasts and voicings. "Dead Man Blues," from the second session, incorporated some spoken intros and special effects. "Grandpa's Spells," from the third session, was unique in its instrumental voicings. In later sessions he recorded "Sidewalk Blues" and "Billy Goat Stomp."

The mid twenties in Chicago turned out to be Morton's heyday. When it became obvious that New York was becoming a musical hub, he moved there in 1928. It was a tough transition. Morton had developed a style that was compatible with small ensembles, but didn't jibe with the developing trend of big bands. Morton tried varied and larger instrumentation, but the recordings were not as polished or successful as the early Victor sessions, although some, such as "Kansas City Stomp," did retain the earlier flavor. There were other highlights of these later sessions as well: "Wolverine Blues," "Mr. Jelly-Lord" and "Shreveport Stomp."

In the early thirties, when his contract was not renewed by Victor, Morton's recording career came to an end. However, several of his tunes were recorded by major artists of the day, including Glenn Miller, Harry James, Fletcher Henderson, Tommy and Jimmy Dorsey and Benny Goodman.

In 1936, Morton moved to Washington, D.C., where he managed and performed in a small nightclub, the Jungle. There, in 1938, he was knifed during a fight, worsening his already deteriorating health. On a brighter note, Alan Lomax's five-week recording session with Morton documenting his music plus an oral history for the Library of Congress, put him back in the limelight during 1938: He was featured on national radio shows, released solo recordings ("Mister Joe") and saw the reissue of some of his earlier recordings.

Ironically, the first song Morton recorded, "King Porter Stomp" (and perhaps his best known), was also the last, recorded on a radio broadcast. In ill health, Morton traveled back to the benign climate of Los Angeles in 1940, and died there from heart failure and asthma on July 10, 1941.

Morton billed himself as the "inventor of jazz." What set Morton apart was that he broke away from the structure of blues and ragtime to invent a new sound and a variety of ways to produce and improvise on it. Many of his tunes, especially "Chicago Breakdown," "King Porter Stomp," "Milenberg Joys" and "Wolverine Blues," became jazz standards to be played and enjoyed with each new generation of jazz musicians and devotees.

*Lomax, Alan. *Mister Jelly Roll: The Fortunes of Jelly Roll Morton New Orleans Creole and "Inventor of Jazz"* (New York, Grove Press).

BUFFALO BLUES

By FERDINAND "JELLY ROLL" MORTON

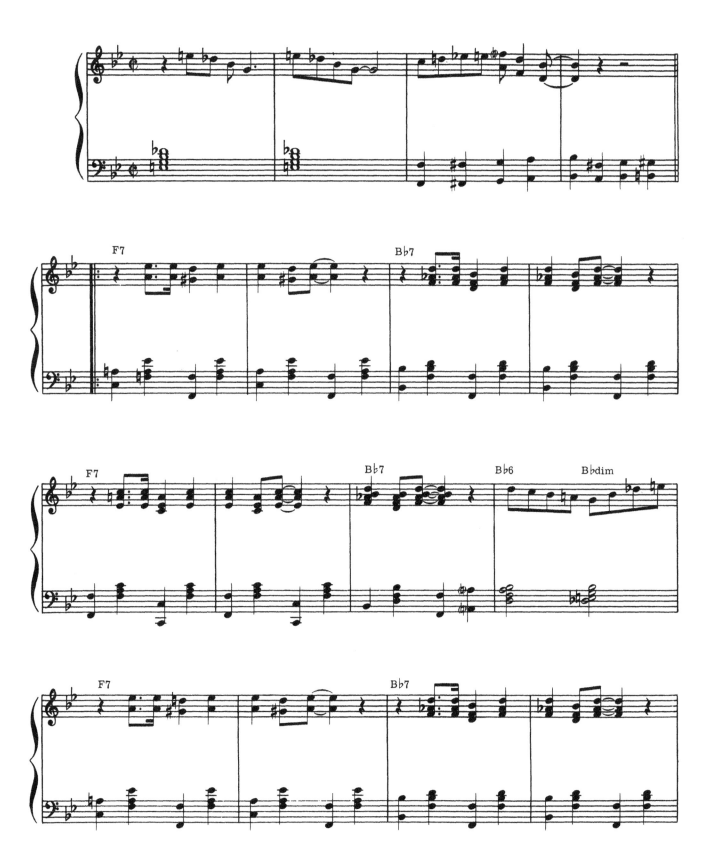

4

BILLY GOAT STOMP

By FERDINAND "JELLY ROLL" MORTON

CHICAGO BREAKDOWN
(a.k.a. Stratford Hunch)

By FERDINAND "JELLY ROLL" MORTON

DEAD MAN BLUES

By FERDINAND "JELLY ROLL" MORTON

FROG-I-MORE RAG
(a.k.a. Froggie More/Sweetheart O'Mine)

By FERDINAND "JELLY ROLL" MORTON

FREAKISH

By FERDINAND "JELLY ROLL" MORTON

GRANDPA'S SPELLS

By FERDINAND "JELLY ROLL" MORTON

JELLY ROLL BLUES
(a.k.a. Original Jelly Roll Blues/Chicago Blues)

By FERDINAND "JELLY ROLL" MORTON

KANSAS CITY STOMP
(a.k.a. Kansas City Stomps)

By FERDINAND "JELLY ROLL" MORTON

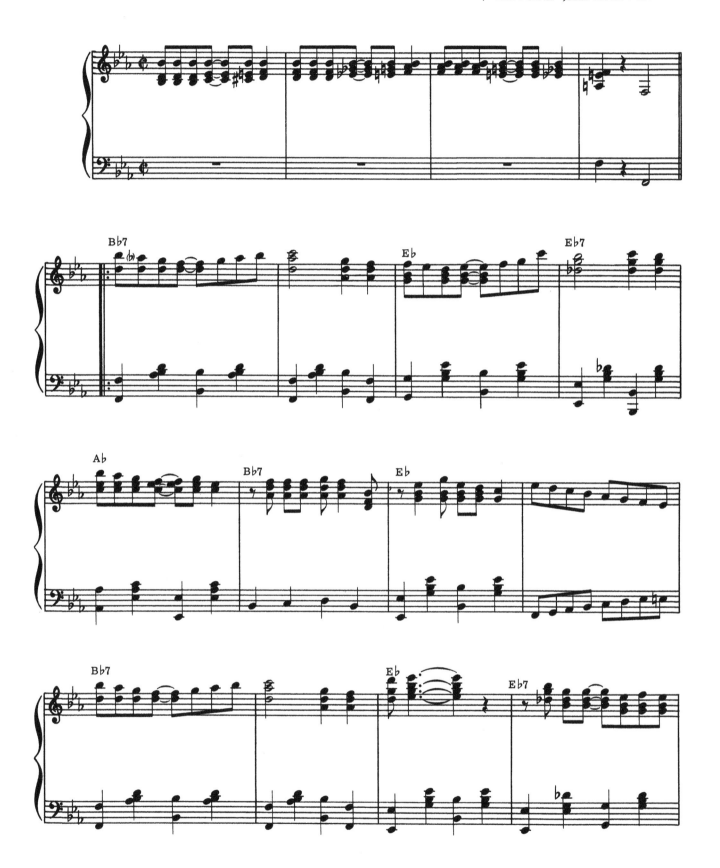

NEW ORLEANS BLUES

By FERDINAND "JELLY ROLL" MORTON

KING PORTER STOMP

Music by FERDINAND "JELLY ROLL" MORTON

LONDON BLUES
(a.k.a. Shoe Shiner's Drag/London Café Blues)

By FERDINAND "JELLY ROLL" MORTON

MILENBERG JOYS

Music by LEON ROPPOLO, PAUL MARES
and FERDINAND "JELLY ROLL" MORTON

MR. JELLY-LORD

By FERDINAND "JELLY ROLL" MORTON

THE PEARLS

By FERDINAND "JELLY ROLL" MORTON

QUEEN OF SPADES
(a.k.a. Black Bottom Stomp)

By FERDINAND "JELLY ROLL" MORTON

SHREVEPORT STOMP

By FERDINAND "JELLY ROLL" MORTON

SIDEWALK BLUES

By FERDINAND "JELLY ROLL" MORTON

TED LEWIS BLUES
(a.k.a. Wild Man Blues)

By FERDINAND "JELLY ROLL" MORTON
and LOUIS ARMSTRONG

WOLVERINE BLUES
(a.k.a. The Wolverines)

By FERDINAND "JELLY ROLL" MORTON